ARE YOU A GENIUS OF LOVE?

Does true love make you look younger? Is love blind? Are couples who live together happier than married couples? Do women fall in love more frequently than men? Does the pursuit of a career hurt a relationship? What is the sexiest gift of clothing you can buy your lover? When does the average American experience his or her first "serious" love? Do women usually initiate flirting? Is one of the best lover's gifts something shaped like a heart? Is sex more important than love? Is nationality important in selecting a mate? Do married people live longer than single people?

LOVERS QUOTIENT TELLS ALL!

LOVERS QUOTIENT

by

Nancy Biracree

PaperJacks LTD.

TORONTO   NEW YORK

AN ORIGINAL

PaperJacks

LOVERS QUOTIENT

PaperJacks LTD.

330 STEELCASE RD. E., MARKHAM, ONT. L3R 2M1
210 FIFTH AVE., NEW YORK, N.Y. 10010

PaperJacks edition published February 1987

ISBN 0-7701-0546-7
Printed in Canada

Table of Contents

LOVERS
QUOTIENT

Life without love is a tomb.

—Robert Browning

There is only one happiness in life,
to love and be loved.

—George Sand

This book is an unabashed celebration of that "happiness" — romance and hearts and flowers and candlelight dinners and walking hand in hand on the beach at sunset and all the other gooey, gorgeous, sentimental stuff of love letters, love stories, and love poetry. It's a recognition that love is the one treasure in life that is available to every human being; no amount of money or fame can buy a person a love any richer than that available to you and to me. It's a call for everyone to cherish love and their lovers as the center of their emotional lives, to value their love as highly as that of Romeo and Juliet, Antony and Cleopatra, and all the other famous lovers of fable and fact.

This celebration is especially important now. In our so-called sophisticated age many of us who admit the need for romance in our lives have often felt uneasy expressing that need in public, as if one of those four-letter words people don't use in polite company is *love*. So hesitant are we to express affection even in writing that only one out of four birthday cards — and one out of six birthday cards for men — even mentions "love." Use the word frequently, and you're called naïve, frivolous, simple, or weak.

But suppose some magician could wave a magic wand and transport all those tens of millions of cynics to a place where they were forced to stand in one of three lines. The first line would commit them to a life without material success; the second line would strip from them physical beauty; and the third line would make the rest of their lives devoid of love.

It is a certainty that the nobody who wasn't crazy would choose the third line, for even the most greedy and the most vain among us would sacrifice anything to avoid a life without love and its wonderful attendant virtues — tenderness, compassion, caring, sharing, relating. The importance of love to everyone's life is pointed out in a wonderful old fable narrated by Leo Buscaglia in his book *Loving Each Other*:

> A young girl is walking through a meadow when she sees a butterfly impaled upon a thorn. Very carefully she releases it and the butterfly starts to fly away. Then it comes back and changes into a beautiful good fairy.
>
> "For your kindness," she tells the little girl, "I will grant you your fondest wish."
>
> The little girl thinks for a moment and replies, "I want to be happy." The fairy leans toward her and whispers in her ear and then suddenly vanishes.
>
> As the girl grew, no one in the land was more happy than she. Whenever anyone asked her for the secret of her happiness, she would only smile and say, "I listened to a good fairy."
>
> As she grew quite old, the neighbors were afraid the fabulous secret might die with her. "Tell us, please," they begged, "tell us what the fairy said."

The now lovely old lady simply smiled and
said, "She told me that everyone, no matter
how secure they seemed, had need of me!"

That need has never been more apparent than today,
as we look back and survey the wreckage of two decades
dominated by what the popular press has called the
"me" generation. This damage includes a 60% divorce
rate, one out of four children being raised by a single
parent, higher-than-ever suicide rates, and a virtual
epidemic of sexually transmitted diseases that threaten
the reproductive health of two generations of women.

It is true that the "sexual revolution" was in some
ways a necessary shedding of outdated values, especially the "double standards" that denied women a
right to a healthy sex life — it turned into an obsession
with sex. Only in the last few years have researchers
come to the forefront to make the case that we have
genetically imprinted in us a "love drive" that's far
stronger and more important than the "sex drive."

Anthropologists tell us that love was vital in the
evolution of the human race. Every species of animal
shares with man the sex drive that leads to the act
of procreation. But only man has the "love drive" that
kept even primitive couples together afterward — during pregnancy, the long period of child rearing, and
on into the even longer period of time to the eve of
death. So imprinted in our genes is love that the emotion releases chemicals inside us that bathe our brains
to produce feelings of euphoria and tranquility.

The vital importance of love in every single person's
life has always been known to the most sensitive of
human beings, the poets, writers, and philosophers
since the dawn of recorded time. Love and romance

are prominent subjects among the earliest fragments of writing of the most ancient civilizations. Love dominated the epics of the ancient Greeks, the poetry of the mighty Roman Empire, the philosophers of the Middle Ages, and the works of great playwrights like Shakespeare in Elizabethan times.

Unfortunately, from the beginning of history until the present day, the political, social, and economic preoccupation of mankind has been with conquest and domination, not love and sharing. Because few dared to seem weak, foolish, or — in a world dominated by males — "unmanly," love was not allowed to cross over the line from private life to public policy.

Now is the time for that to change. Our obsession with conquest and power and wealth has brought us to the brink of nuclear disaster, as well as threatening to shatter the traditional family that condemns large groups of people to live out their lives in loneliness and despair. As never before we need to acknowledge the importance of our love drive, our need for each other.

The way to do that is a "love revolution" that brings romance "out of the bedroom" in the same way that the sexual revolution removed so much of the unnecessary embarrassment connected with sex. We need love education courses — as well as sex education courses — in our schools. We need universities to create departments of love, with tenured love professors. We need a magazine called *Love* to join *Time* and *Money* on the newsstands.

Finally, we need to elevate Valentine's Day, the celebration of love and romance, to the status of a major holiday. This elevation will signal the liberation of our need to love, just as the Fourth of July celebrates the liberation of our country.

Love understands love; it needs no talk.

—Francis Ridley Havergal

How do we begin the "love revolution?" A good place to start is by shattering the myth that love is all emotion, all mysterious feelings and glances that just "happens" to two people and just as mystically disappears. If that were true, there would be absolutely nothing anyone could do to increase his/her chances of enjoying a long-lasting and loving relationship other than waiting helplessly for "luck" to bestow love on him/her.

Nothing could be further from the truth. Love is not a magical "something," but rather the highest order of human relationship. Just as there is a body of knowledge about other human relationships — parent-child, employer-employee, buyer-seller — there is a huge body of knowledge about love. The more you know about love, the better your chance of finding and sustaining a life-enriching loving relationship. There are people who are geniuses at love, just as there are geniuses in every other aspect of human life.

Chances are you already know more about love than you think. This book gives you the opportunity to find out exactly how expert you are by giving you an *LQ*, a "Lovers Quotient," just as you have an IQ. You may find out you're one of those geniuses at love!

If you're not, however, don't despair. It's a lot easier to raise your *LQ* to genius level than your IQ. Within the answers to the questions of the *LQ* quiz, you'll find such vital information as:

- 130 facts about love
- 130 ways to tell if it's true love
- 130 ways to say "I love you"
- 130 ways to make love last

Where does this information come from? From the experts at love, who include not only psychologists, sociologists, and marriage counselors, but also poets, writers, philosophers, and great lovers themselves. This book includes not only questions, checklists, facts, and techniques, but quotes and statements about love that you can weigh against the stirrings of your own heart.

The *LQ* test is meant to be taken not once, but several times over the course of a lifetime. As your knowledge of love grows, so will the depth of your loving relationship. The higher your *LQ*, the more you will realize that the possibilities for love are as endless as the far reaches of the universe, yet are as near at hand as your own heart.

What's Your LQ?
Part One: How Much Do You Know About the Facts of Love?

Were it not for love, life would not be a
ship worth the launching.

—Edward Arlington Robinson

One valuable way to understand love is to think of
it as another natural resource vital to our existence,
like the air we breathe and the water we drink. Almost
every man and woman alive knows that life is impossible without oxygen and water. Yet for generations
in this country, our relentless obsession with progress
— including building bigger factories, faster cars, more
powerful bombs — polluted our precious natural
resources to a point where our existence was in jeopardy if this pollution continued apace. Only recently
have we come to our senses enough to begin to purify
our environment.

Romantic love is the source of the most
intense delights that life has to offer.

—Bertrand Russell

In the last three decades, love has been polluted,

too, and chief among the causes has been an obsession with sex. Sex is, of course, an important expression of love and passion and a prime pleasure of life. But from what we've read and heard and seen from the media in the last three decades, one can't help but think that *all* that's vital in the relationship between man and woman is how, how often, and how well they "do it."

The reason for this avalanche of books and movies and television shows and magazine articles and newspaper accounts is that sex makes a better "story" than love. Sex is "trendy," "sophisticated," "titillating," even "naughty." Love, on the other hand, is "old-fashioned," "passé," "dull," even "boring."

We receive love — not in proportion to our demands or sacrifices or needs, but roughly in proportion to our own capacity to love.

—Rollo May

The end result of the media attention on sex is that most of us know a lot more about the "facts of life" than we do about the facts of love. Without solid facts, we tend to believe what we read: "everybody's getting divorced"; "nobody wants to get married"; "everybody's career is more important than their family." Ignorance and misinformation inevitably lead to a pessimistic attitude that severely diminishes our own capacity to love. And, as Rollo May points out, our own capacity to love is the key factor in the kind of love we get.

Fortunately, the true facts of love in North America will no doubt put a smile on your face and a glow in your heart. We're waking up to the dangers of love pollution, just as we woke up to the dangers of air and water pollution. Wouldn't it be wonderful if, as part of the "love revolution," a new Department of Love Protection was organized to help safeguard the most important of our emotional resources?

Love is the mutuality of devotion forever subduing the antagonism of divided function.

—Erik Erikson

Following is the first part of the *LQ* quiz, which tests your knowledge of the facts of love. Even if you get all the answers right, you'll find hundreds of facts in the answers that are guaranteed to fill your heart with new optimism about the power and possibilities of love.

QUIZ QUESTIONS

T F 1. When asked, "What do you look for in a relationship?," more Americans replied "good sex" than "love."

T F 2. When asked, "What is your greatest source of satisfaction?," twice as many Americans answered "children and marriage" than answered "my job."

T F 3. Many more say sex is very important for a happy life than say love is important for a happy life.

T F 4. Out of fourteen reasons for marriage, Americans ranked "having another person to share one's life" as number 1.

T F 5. 95% of Americans marry at some point in their lives.

T F 6. Fewer than half of divorced people ever remarry.

T F 7. 85% of Americans are satisfied with their marriage.

T F 8. Only 50% of married people would take the same spouse if they had to do it over again.

T F 9. Couples who live together are generally happier than married couples.

T F 10. One out of four newly married couples will celebrate their 40th wedding anniversary.

T F 11. More than 50% of today's college students approve of extramarital affairs.

T F 12. The divorce rate will be higher for women now in their twenties than for women now in their thirties.

T F 13. More people meet their future mates at singles bars or through dating services than by any other means.

T F 14. The average American experiences his or her first "serious" love at age seventeen.

People think love is emotion. Love is good sense.

—Ken Kesey

T F 15. When asked, "What feature most attracts you to a person's face?," 66% of Americans answered "hair."

T F 16. Women rate a man's top physical attribute as "his face."

T F 17. Men rate a woman's top physical attribute as "her bust."

T F 18. More women appreciate a man's achievements than his athletic ability.

T F 19. More men appreciate a woman's social skills than her physical attractiveness.

T F 20. 50% more men than women consider themselves "better than average" looking.

T F 21. 66% of the time, a woman initiates flirting.

T   F   22. The most common mistake a man makes when first meeting a woman is moving too slowly.

T   F   23. Most men prefer "hard to get" women.

T   F   24. Women fall in love more frequently than men.

T   F   25. Women fall in love more quickly than men.

T   F   26. Americans fall in love an average of twice in a lifetime.

T   F   27. More women than men have "played dumb" on a date.

T   F   28. When asked to rank the most important ingredients of love, more people mention "sexual electricity" than "friendship."

T   F   29. People who tend to fall in love very easily are less likely to suffer a broken marriage.

T   F   30. Over 80% of Americans marry a person of the same religion.

Life is a flower of which love is the honey.

—Victor Hugo

T F 31. 50% of Americans marry someone of the same ethnic background.

T F 32. Over 50% of all couples who marry today have first lived together.

T F 33. The women most dissatisfied with their marriages are those who married for reasons other than love.

T F 34. The average couple spends half their free time together.

T F 35. The more money you make, the closer your marriage is likely to be.

T F 36. Very attractive people have happier marriages than those whose looks are just average.

T F 37. Married men and women live longer than men and women living by themselves.

QUIZ ANSWERS

1. FALSE

This statement couldn't be more wrong. When asked, "What do you look for in a relationship?," 53% of Americans say love, 32% say companionship, and only 1% answer sex. Almost all of us — 96%, to be exact — feel that romance is very important to our lives, and 75% of us believe that newspapers, television, and movies put far too much emphasis on sex and not enough on love and romance.

2. **TRUE**

Over 80% of us list our children and marriage as a "great source of satisfaction." No other aspect of our lives — friends, sex, job — was rated greatly satisfying by as many as two out of five of us.

Lovers represent a world in us, a world possibly not born until they arrive, and it is only by this meeting that a new world is born.

—Anaïs Nin

Almost every other survey of adult Americans, married or single, affirms that "old-fashioned" values like love, romance, and family are by far our most important values. Eighty-six percent of Americans rate having a traditional marriage a "most important" life goal. And 92% of married Americans say that their family is in fact the "most important" thing in their lives.

3. **FALSE**

You may think single men are all wolves, but studies show most are just lambs in wolf's clothing. Eighty-five percent of men rate love as "very important for a happy satisfied life," while only 48% place that much importance on sex. Eighty-three percent of women and 77% of men say that in relationships love must come before sex.

4. TRUE

To paraphrase the song, Americans are most of all "people who need people." Of fourteen reasons for marriage, only two were rated "very important" by Americans: 1. "having another person to share one's life" (mentioned by 74%); and 2. "having another person to share important life experiences" (67%).

5. TRUE

Surprised? You may well be, after all you've read about the legions of smart sophisticated people who revel in the independence of being unmarried and unburdened by family ties. You'd think marriage is passé.

> One cannot be strong without love. For love is not an irrelevant emotion; it is the blood of life.
>
> —Paul Tillich

It is true that people are waiting to marry later — the average marriage age for men is now twenty-five, and the average age for women is twenty-three. It's also true that among certain demographic groups — the 25% of young women who are college graduates, for example — as many as 10% may remain unmarried. Still, 2,500,000 Americans married in 1985, an increase of 16% over 1975. The marriage rate in 1985 was the highest since 1950.

The following table, the marital status of Americans by age and sex, shows how popular matrimony really is:

Male

Age	% Single	% Married	% Divorced	% Widowed
18–19	96.8	3.1	.1	—
20–24	74.8	23.5	1.6	.1
25–29	37.8	56.7	5.3	.1
30–34	20.9	69.8	9.1	.1
35–39	11.6	78.2	9.8	.4
40–44	6.9	82.6	10.2	.3
45–54	6.2	84.2	8.5	1.1
55–64	5.4	85.2	5.8	3.6
65–74	5.5	81.9	3.7	8.9
75+	4.0	70.1	2.0	23.8

Female

Age	% Single	% Married	% Divorced	% Widowed
18–19	87.1	12.4	.5	—
20–24	56.9	39.4	3.6	.1
25–29	25.9	65.5	7.9	.6
30–34	13.3	74.2	11.6	.8
35–39	7.5	77.4	13.6	1.4
40–44	5.4	77.6	13.9	3.0
45–54	4.6	78.5	10.8	6.0
55–64	4.2	69.4	8.9	17.5
65–74	5.0	50.7	5.2	39.1
75+	6.5	23.9	2.7	66.9

6. FALSE

Marriage is so important to our lives that even after one failure, 84% of men and 79% of women try again. Only 58% of all marriages involve two people who've never been married before. Twenty-one percent of Americans have been married two or more times.

7. **TRUE**

The vast majority of Americans consider their marriages happy, even though more than six in ten married people say they at least occasionally have trouble getting along with their spouses.

8. **FALSE**

A *Psychology Today* magazine study revealed that 88% of men and 80% of women say they would take the same partner again, if they had to do it all over again.

9. **FALSE**

Friendship is love without wings.

—Lord Byron

A number of independent studies show that married couples are much happier than nonmarried cohabiting couples. One study conducted by *Psychology Today* suggested that the reason couples that live together are less satisfied with their relationships is that they are more insecure and tend to be more jealous than married couples.

10. **TRUE**

Of all newly married couples:

- 63% will celebrate their 10th anniversary.
- 41% will celebrate their 25th anniversary.
- 25% will celebrate their 40th anniversary.
- 13% will celebrate their 50th anniversary.

In 1986, more than 50,000 couples celebrated their Golden Wedding Anniversary.

11. FALSE

Only 13% of today's college students approve of extra-marital affairs, an indication of a profound return to "traditional" values among young people. When high school and college students ranked the most important factors in life, they placed "loving and being loved" as number 1. One-third of today's college students think their parents' generation was too promiscuous, and only 19% approve of "one-night stands." The percentage of high school juniors and seniors who'd like to be virgins when they're married jumped from 11% to 26% in the last ten years, and the number who've had sex dropped from 40% to 25%.

12. FALSE

The soaring divorce rates you've been reading about peak among women now in their late thirties. For the last two years, the divorce rate has dropped sharply and the U.S. Census Bureau predicts that 10% fewer marriages involving women now in their twenties will end in divorce.

Love is not getting, but giving. It is sacrifice. If a person is worth loving at all, they are worth loving generously, even recklessly.

—Marie Dressier

---

13. **FALSE**

Surveys have shown that the most common places people meet their future mates are, in order:

1. Family — family gatherings, friends of family members, meetings with distant relatives.
2. Work — colleagues or their friends.
3. Education — high school, college, or adult education courses.
4. Leisure activities — theater, sports, concerts, art exhibitions.
5. Social gatherings — parties, singles groups, weddings, bars.
6. Community action — church, local politics, charity work.
7. Dating and marriage bureaus.
8. Travel — tours, cruises, singles resorts.
9. Chance encounters — supermarkets, laundromats, department stores.
10. Newspaper advertisements.

14. **TRUE**

The average American experiences his or her first "puppy" love at age thirteen, then has the first serious love four years later.

15. **FALSE**

When asked "What feature most attracts you to a person's face?," Americans replied:

Eyes	62%
Hair	22%

Teeth	5%
Mouth	3%
Other	8%

16. **TRUE**

Women rated a man's top attribute as:

Face	55%
Hair	8%
Shoulders	7%
Chest	6%
Hands	4%

17. **FALSE**

Men rated a woman's top attribute as:

Face	32%
Legs	24%
Bust	18%
Hair	5%
Buttocks	4%

Ah, better to love in the lowliest cottage
than pine in a palace alone.

—G. J. Whyte-Melville

---

18. **TRUE**

The qualities women most appreciate in men are, in order:

1. Achievement
2. Leadership

3. Occupational ability
4. Economic ability
5. Entertaining ability
6. Intellectual ability
7. Observational ability
8. Common sense
9. Athletic ability
10. Theoretical ability

19. **FALSE**

The qualities men most appreciate in women are, in order:

1. Physical attractiveness
2. Erotic ability
3. Affectional ability
4. Social skills
5. Domestic ability
6. Sartorial ability
7. Interpersonal understanding
8. Art appreciation
9. Moral-spiritual understanding
10. Art-creative ability

20. **TRUE**

Men, on the average, have a much better opinion of their looks than do women. Below are two tables that give the results of people being asked to describe how they looked to others:

Men responded as follows:

Extremely handsome	5%

Very attractive	9%
Attractive	28%
Average good looks	33%
Interesting-looking	11%
Plain	6%
Uncertain	8%

Women responded as follows:

Very beautiful	3%
Very attractive	12%
Pretty	13%
Average good looks	47%
Interesting-looking	12%
Plain	4%
Uncertain	9%

21. **TRUE**

Women do initiate the majority of flirting, and they direct the early part of what sociologists call the "courtship sequence" — approach, talk, touch — which lasts from fifteen minutes to three hours. About 20% of the time, women end up asking men for a date.

Love will find its way, through paths where wolves would fear to prey.

—Lord Byron

---

22. **FALSE**

The most common mistake men make is moving too quickly. The reason is, as the answer to the previous question indicates, that women like to feel in charge of flirting and meeting.

The reason men move too quickly is that they often misread body language. Of the total feeling expressed by a spoken message, only 7% is verbal feeling, 38% is vocal feeling, and 55% is conveyed by facial expression. Signs of encouragement from a person of the opposite sex include:

1. Eyebrows raised
2. Eyes wide open, prolonged eye contact
3. Mouth open and smiling
4. Lips moistened more often with tongue
5. Nods of head in agreement
6. Body inclined toward other person
7. Expressive hand gestures
8. Small touching movements

There is also a definite sequence of physical contact in the "mating ritual." The stages are:

1. Eye to body
2. Eye to eye
3. Voice to voice
4. Hand to hand
5. Arm to shoulder
6. Arm to waist
7. Mouth to mouth
8. Hand to head
9. Hand to body
10. Mouth to breast
11. Hand to genitals
12. Genitals to genitals

23. FALSE

Neither men nor women are generally attracted to aloof people of the opposite sex. Men in particular find out-going, friendly women the most desirable. When asked the first thing they noticed about their lovers, more than twice as many Americans named "a smile" than any other attribute. Several other studies have shown that the most effective opening "lines" are simple, innocuous statements such as, "Hi, my name is..."; "Nice place, isn't it?"; and, "That's a pretty dress/ handsome suit you're wearing."

24. TRUE

Women fall in love more frequently, but they also end about 70% of all relationships. Women and men, however, have about the same number of unrequited loves. Twelve percent of both men and women have had three or more one-sided loves.

O, there is nothing holier, in this life of ours, than the first consciousness of love — the first fluttering of its silken wings.

—Henry Wadsworth Longfellow

---

25. FALSE

Men fall in love more quickly than women, and they hang on longer when a love affair dies.

On the average, about 20% of men say they fall in

love by the fourth date, about 30% say it takes at least twenty dates, and the rest fall somewhere in between.

26. FALSE

Americans fall in love an average of six times during their lives. Women believe that true love happens an average of once in a lifetime, while men believe that it occurs an average of twice.

27. TRUE

Thirty-one percent of men admit to having played dumb, compared with 23% of women.

28. FALSE

When asked to rate the most important ingredients of love, Americans rank friendship, devotion, and intellectual compatibility above sexual electricity, irrational longing, and mysterious chemistry.

There's also another strange element that seems to strengthen love, and that's what your parents name you. People whose first names begin with the same letter (e.g. Mickey and Minnie Mouse) are 12% more likely to marry than couples whose names begin with different letters.

29. FALSE

About 25% of Americans are "love prone," having fallen in love at least twelve times, while another 21% are almost "love prone" (having fallen in love eight to eleven times). The divorce rate for "love prone" people is 60% higher than that of others who fall in love less easily.

> In the last analysis, love is only the reflection of a person's own worthiness from other people.
>
> —Ralph Waldo Emerson

---

30. TRUE

Religion still plays a very large part in our lives and our marriages; 78% of first marriages and 60% of remarriages are religious ceremonies. And religion is still an important factor in choosing a marriage partner:

- 91% of Protestant men marry Protestant women.
- 82% of Catholic men marry Catholic women.
- 85% of Jewish men marry Jewish women.

Another important factor is education. Of all marriages:

- 55% are between people of the same educational level.
- 26% include husbands with more education.
- 19% include wives with more education.

31. FALSE

Unlike religion, ethnic background plays far less of

a role in selecting a mate than it did half a century ago.

- 27% of marriages are between people of entirely the same ethnic background.
- 26% are between people of partially overlapping ethnic background.
- 47% are between people of entirely different ethnic backgrounds.

One factor that hasn't changed is age; 74% of women still marry older men, compared with 14% that marry younger men.

32. TRUE

In the last ten years, the percentage of couples who've lived together before marriage has jumped from 13% to 53%.

33. TRUE

Women who marry for reasons other than love are more dissatisfied, and the most dissatisfied of all are women who marry because they are pregnant. According to a Roper Poll, Americans believe the most important factors in a marriage are:

	Men	Women
Being in love	89%	91%
Fidelity	83%	77%
Keeping romance alive	74%	75%
Good sexual relationship	72%	69%
Financial security	53%	58%
Children	45%	46%

Factors other than love that researchers have found to be less conducive to a happy marriage are:

- One partner very much more interested in sports
- One partner very much taller
- Man more interested in fine arts and music
- Man in need of more affection
- Man's thinking more abstract
- One very dominant, the other very submissive
- Man much more tense

On the other hand, factors besides love that researchers have found to be conducive to happiness are:

- Couple similarly sober or happy-go-lucky
- Couple similarly confident or apprehensive
- One witty; other placid

34. TRUE

Married couples still spend a majority of their time together. However, when men and women were asked to recall the most interesting conversations they had that day, married people mentioned conversations with others three times more often than they mentioned conversations with their spouse.

35. TRUE

Surprisingly, upper-class couples tend to have closer marriages than middle-class couples, who in turn are closer than lower-class couples. Also, couples closer in social class tend to be happier:

- 53% of marriages between partners of the same social class are rated good.
- 35% of marriages between partners one social class apart are rated good.
- 14% of marriages between partners two social classes apart are rated good.

36. FALSE

The more attractive a married person is, the more competitive he/she feels with a spouse, and the more he/she resents attention paid to the spouse.

Yet what is love, good shepard, saint? It is a sunshine mixed with rain.

—Sir Walter Raleigh

---

37. TRUE
Married men, on the average, live four years longer than single men. Married women whose husbands are alive live longer than widows.

Part Two: How Much Do You Know About True Love?

After all the storybook romances we've been exposed to in our formative years, there are very few of us who don't feel uncomfortable even asking, "Is this true love?" Aren't we just supposed to "know" true love after a glance, a touch, or perhaps a whirlwind court-ship? Then aren't we supposed to forget about questions entirely and enjoy living "happily ever after"?

The problem is, as all of us eventually discover, love isn't a fixed concept but an ever-changing relationship between two ever-changing people living in an ever-changing world. And the question "Is this my true love?" is one that can ultimately and finally be answered in retrospect, after the relationship has been put to the test of time.

Let no one who loves be called unhappy. Even love unreturned has its rainbow.

—Sir James Matthew Barrie

The impossibility of arriving at a "perfect" answer, however, doesn't mean that we should abandon reason and search for love only with our hearts. Rather, research has shown that the happiest people are those who've made "educated" choices, blending their past experiences and whatever they can learn from experts.

Who are these experts at love? Since love involves the heart as well as the head, they include poets, writers, philosophers, and other lovers, as well as psychologists, marriage counselors, and sociologists. The "experiences" they provide range from concrete questions to ask and checklists to follow, to reflections about true love to read and ponder against the emotions swelling in your heart.

The second part of the *LQ* quiz that follows not only tests your knowledge of what constitutes true love, but also acts as a valuable "study guide" that can vastly increase your awareness of the intricate process of developing relationships. And the usefulness of this awareness doesn't end once you've made a "big" decision like committing yourself to matrimony. Marriage isn't a destination, but a landmark in a lifetime voyage across seas that can often be buffetted by storms. The most successful navigators on this course are those who take the time to stop and recheck their positions against the "chart" of true love they've established as the goal in their relationship.

QUIZ QUESTIONS

T F 38. The best candidate for marriage is a partner who has always needed someone to live with him/her.

T F 39. It's unromantic to evaluate your prospective partner as objectively as if he/she were applying for a job.

Adam could not be happy even in
paradise without Eve.

—Sir John Lubbock

T F 40. True love makes you look younger.

T F 41. One way to tell it's true love is that you
find yourself and your lover doing crazy
things you've never done before.

T F 42. The surest way to douse the flame of love
is to ask your lover to compare you with
others of the same sex.

T F 43. True love says, "I love you because I
need you."

T F 44. True love transcends such mundane mat-
ters as how much money your lover
spends or how generous he/she is.

T F 45. A relationship is headed for trouble
when lovers don't agree on the definition
of success.

T F 46. The best lover is one who looks at life
with a tough, realistic eye and always
prepares for the worst.

T F 47. A lover who expresses a lot of tolerance
for the sexual promiscuity of others is a
poor risk as a life partner.

T F 48. A person who often says "I'm not good enough for you" is probably right.

T F 49. Marriages work better when one partner is firmly in charge.

T F 50. The course of true love is easier when two people prefer the same pace of life.

T F 51. Beware of a lover who occasionally acts like a child.

T F 52. It's immature love when you find yourself daydreaming about your partner.

T F 53. An ideal lover is a person who is the embodiment of sophistication.

T F 54. Love is not "blind" — infatuation is blind.

T F 55. A true lover is a reliable psychological mirror, a way to see ourself through the responses of a person we care for.

T F 56. There's one right person in this world for everyone.

It is best to love wisely, no doubt, but to love foolishly is better than not to be able to love at all.

—William Makepeace Thackeray

T F 57. The ideal partner is a person who can fulfill all of your needs.

T F 58. Your life partner should be a person with the internal resources that allow him/her not to be bowled over by the normal difficulties and obstacles of life.

T F 59. You should try to marry a person adaptable enough to live by the philosophy "When in Rome, do as the Romans do."

T F 60. A danger signal in a relationship is finding yourself saying, "I'll do anything to keep him/her."

T F 61. One of the marks of true love is placing your lover on a pedestal.

T F 62. The best relationships are those in which both partners have serious interests outside the relationship, including meaningful personal friendships.

T F 63. It's infatuation rather than true love if separation causes genuine despair.

T F 64. A woman can tell it's true love when she thinks he's as sexy as Paul Newman, as athletic as Pete Rose, as selfless and dedicated as Ralph Nader, as smart as John Kenneth Galbraith, and as funny as Don Rickles.

T F 65. The best real-life loves are those that

match the traditional "Christian" view of love as undemanding, patient, kind, and ever present.

T F 66. One sign that you may be ready for a long-lasting relationship is sexual frustration.

T F 67. The course of even the longest-lasting loves includes a time when both partners feel bored, impatient, frustrated, and hurt.

T F 68. You should always try to banish from your mind any negative thoughts about your lover.

T F 69. One measure of how serious your lover is is how seriously he/she takes Valentine's Day.

Love is something eternal — the aspect may change, but not the essence.

—Vincent van Gogh

T F 70. Beware of any hint of jealousy on the part of your prospective partner.

T F 71. If you find yourself afraid of intimacy from time to time, it's a sign your relationship is in trouble.

T   F   72. Before you commit yourself wholly to
another person, you should ask yourself,
"Is he/she really different from the ones
who have come before?"

QUIZ ANSWERS

38. FALSE

Bertrand Russell once said, "To fear love is to fear
life — and those who fear life are already three-quarters
dead." The people who are afraid of life are those
who lack the self-reliance to live alone, and that dependency places great strains on a relationship. Only those
who have lived well alone can live well with another.

39. FALSE

As novelist Ken Kesey has commented, "People think
love is just emotion. Love is good sense." Marriage
is the most rational way for two adults to live their
lives, and choosing a partner should be a rational decision. It would be foolish not to take a look at the
same kind of things an employer checks before hiring
— for example, a person's credit history, honesty,
responsibility in fulfilling the obligations of a job.

40. TRUE

Love is a mirror in which you behold yourself. Take
a peek at how your love looks on you. Are you happy
with what you see? Do you look younger? Do you
sport a spontaneous smile? Do you radiate a new
energy?

41. TRUE

It's a fact that true love makes you slightly crazy. The key word, however, is *slightly*. Many lovers take a new delight in playful zaniness, like dancing in a fountain at 2 A.M. But truly crazy behavior that plunges a lover into debt or places his/her job into jeopardy is a warning signal.

Be gentle with me, new love. Treat me tenderly. I need the gentle touch, the soft voice, the candlelight after nine.

—Rod McKuen

---

42. FALSE

It's extremely important to find out what your lover really thinks of you. True love is impossible when your partner is faking intimacy to get sex or, on the other hand, has idealized you so much that you're eventually bound to disappoint him/her. Before you make a long-term commitment, you should ask such questions as:

- If there were one thing you could change about me, what would it be?
- In which ways do you think I resemble my mother (father)?
- How much weight do you think I ought to lose?
- Which of my man/woman friends do you regard as the most attractive?
- Under what circumstances would you be unfaithful to me?

43. FALSE

In his great book, *The Art of Loving*, Erich Fromm remarks, "Immature love says, 'I love you because I need you.' Mature love says, 'I need you because I love you.'" What Fromm is saying is that the foundation of true love must be the question, "What can I do for you?," not "What can you do for me?" A mature lover wants a partner to grow and unfold for his/her own sake, and not for the purpose of serving his/her own needs.

44. FALSE

Love may be all hearts and flowers, but in real life nearly three out of four married couples say that the primary subject matter of their arguments is money. Love that is real can't be spoiled by honest discussions of real-life questions such as how to stick to a budget, how to save money, and what gifts should go to friends and relatives.

45. TRUE

It's vitally important for lovers to discuss in detail their fundamental philosophies of life. The three critical questions are:

1. Do we want the same things out of life?
2. Do we agree on the meaning of success?
3. What are your goals? What are mine? Are there conflicts between the two?

46. FALSE

Joy in marriage comes easiest to those who come to

marriage with joy in their hearts. Beware of people with pessimistic attitudes. A person who lives in a world in which almost every door seems closed may be open to the compromise necessary for marriage. While all of us have some negative attitudes, make sure you find a partner who chooses to believe that happy things are at least as much a part of life as unhappy things.

We are all born for love . . . It is the principle of existence.

—Disraeli-Sybil

---

47. **TRUE**

People who are very tolerant of loveless, promiscuous sex tend to have very few qualms about engaging in such behavior themselves. Such partners are very likely to have affairs after marriage. Watch out!

48. **TRUE**

A person who constantly belittles himself/herself probably doesn't have the self-esteem necessary to make mature love work. Falling in love out of sympathy for such a person is one of fourteen common mistakes people make in love that have been identified by psychologist Carol Botwin. These mistakes are:

1. *Falling in love with love:* who can live up to a fantasy that is based on someone else's wishes rather than his/her own characteristics?

2. *Pop the question, please.* People get anxious too early, because of their desire for commitment.

3. *Love as a magic potion.* The attitude is, when the right man or woman comes along, he or she will fix whatever is wrong in our lives.

4. *Rescue me.* One partner feels he/she can rescue the other from alcoholism, depression, *etc.*

5. *Let's talk about it, later.* You can harbor illusions not based on reality by putting off discussions.

6. *True love runs smooth.* All relationships, even very good ones, have their ups and downs. If people don't recognize that, they over-react when conflicts arise.

7. *Swept under the rug.* In the desire to keep things smooth, problems are swept under the rug.

8. *Ringing of chimes.* Mistaking infatuation for real love.

9. *Ignoring the clues.* A person knows himself/herself better than you do. A person who says "I'm not good enough for you" or "I don't want to get involved" probably means it.

10. *Looking for Mr./Mrs. Perfect.* People blame their unhappiness on their current partner rather than on the impossibility they are looking for.

11. *One-sided affair.* Watch out if you find yourself desperately trying to believe, "Someday he/she will love me as much as I love him/her."

12. *The macho man or domineering woman.* People into dominance and control can't tolerate a give-and-take atmosphere. Any attempt to change the power structure is seen as a threat.

13. *Measuring up to ex-mates.* You can never best a rival who isn't there, and partners who want to live in the past have no energy for the present.

14. *Games people play.* People sometimes conduct their affairs as if they were in a war zone — such as trying to make their partner jealous or playing one's emotional cards close to the vest.

Things that are lovely can tear my heart in two — Moonlight on still pools, you.

—Dorothy Dow

---

49. FALSE

The key to love is mutuality. In any relationship where one of the partners is treated as an inferior, honest communication is impossible and building resentment eventually corrupts love.

Mutuality, however, doesn't mean that two people can or should be equal in every area. Sociologists Genevieve Grafe Marcus and Robert Lee Smith have identified ten areas of power that concern couples. Their research has shown that the most successful marriages are those among two people who show a balance of power when all ten areas are added together. Those ten areas are:

1. Physical power (beauty, body, clothes, gender, sexuality, strength).
2. Work/profession/career power.
3. Economic power.
4. Educational power (degrees, cultural attainments, wisdom).
5. Acquired skills (craftsmanship, mechanical and other practical skills, such as cooking, carpentry, *etc.*).
6. Emotional power (the ability to inspire affection and attachment in others, independent of one's own feelings).
7. Intra- and inter-personal power (social skills, charm, warmth, supportiveness).
8. Natural abilities (talent, wit, physical dexterity).
9. Character skills (honesty, loyalty, dependability, perseverance, fairness, cheerfulness, assertiveness).
10. Association power (influential friends or relatives).

50. TRUE

It's always wise to stop in the course of love and compare your pace of life with your lover's. If you always want to linger on a walk to admire the beauty, while your partner is always in a hurry, you may be in trouble.

51. FALSE

All of us need to act like a child at times. Lovers should

always be able to be different selves with each other at different times. Acting like a child is one of those selves. The critical problem comes in a relationship where only one partner can act like a child and only one is always the parent.

Love is the triumph of imagination over intelligence.

—H. L. Mencken

---

52. FALSE

If you don't daydream, then you're not in love. Fantasy is one of the magical parts of true love.

53. FALSE

Sophistication is often the final refuge of people who are frightened of passion, devotion, and commitment, all requirements of true love.

54. TRUE

Far from being blind, mature love is a giant magnifying glass. You should be able to see your lover more clearly than anyone else in the world.

55. TRUE

Love is the ultimate expression of our need for human companionship, for someone to share our values, feelings, interests, and goals, to share the joys and burdens of existence. Sharing means the most with a partner who knows us to the depths of our hearts and responds to our emotional needs appropriately.

56. **FALSE**

If the romantic myth that there is just one right person for each of us were true, we'd have to live for centuries to search among the hundreds of millions of possibilities. More bad marriages have been made because someone was afraid of losing "Mr./Mrs. Right" than for any other reason.

Fortunately, life provides us with a multitude of opportunities for happiness. Anyone with a heart full of love and a positive attitude can and will eventually find another person with whom to form a long-term, productive relationship.

57. **FALSE**

Nothing is more damaging to a long-term relationship than one partner being totally dependent on the other for all of his/her needs. True love is possible only when both partners come to the relationship with self-esteem, the recognition that they each have some needs no other person can fulfill except themselves.

58. **TRUE**

Most of us know enough to be wary of a person who wants to marry "on the rebound" from a broken romance or marriage. But equally dangerous is a person on the rebound from other life crises — a bad relationship with parents, unemployment, drug or alcohol abuse, or even depression. We should all be aware that no one can possibly handle the inevitable difficulties of marriage if he/she can't handle the routine difficulties of life.

> Love is a butterfly, which when pursued is just beyond your grasp, but if you will sit down quietly it may alight upon you.
>
> —Nathaniel Hawthorne

---

59. FALSE

Integrity is an important part of any loving relationship. An important part of integrity is having a firm set of values that you live by, regardless of circumstances. A person whose values and opinions change with the company he/she keeps can't be trusted to keep your relationship whole and sacred.

60. TRUE

True love can't thrive when one partner gives up his/her independence. Your chances for long-term happiness are in danger when you find yourself saying:

- I have to do whatever he/she wants.
- My needs don't count anymore.
- I'll have to turn into a selfless servant like my mother.
- I'll do anything just to keep him/her.
- I'm so scared of rejection I'll sell out.
- I can't face admitting I have needs.
- I've given my partner the power to hurt me.

- I've totally accommodated my life-style to his/hers.

61. FALSE

Statues belong on pedestals, not people. Your relationship is headed for trouble if you act like a sculptor — that is, you try to mold your partner into an idealized image of perfection. But perfection can't exist in life, and idealizing another person can only lead to disappointment. One fundamental requirement of true love is two people recognizing and fully accepting the imperfections in each other.

62. TRUE

There's a big difference between sharing your life with someone and sharing everything in it. No relationship can grow unless there are some open spaces in it for each partner to explore his/her own distinctive needs and interests.

63. FALSE

Such anguish over separation is entirely normal, as psychologist Kenneth Pope's famous definition of romantic love points out:

A preoccupation with another person. A deeply felt desire to be with the loved one. A feeling of incompleteness without him or her. Thinking of the loved one often, whether together or apart. Separation frequently provokes feelings of genuine despair or tantalizing anticipation of reuniting. Reunion is seen as bringing feelings of euphoric ecstasy or peace and fulfillment.

> In jealousy there is more self-love than
> love.
>
> —François, duc de la Rochefoucauld

64. FALSE

Judith Viorst points out that such idealism is a sure sign of infatuation. It's true love when a woman realizes that her lover is actually about as sexy as Don Rickles, as athletic as Ralph Nader, as smart as Pete Rose, as funny as John Kenneth Galbraith, and doesn't resemble Paul Newman in any way — but you'll stick with him anyway.

65. FALSE

This kind of idealized relationship is one of six categories of romantic love developed by sociologist John Alan Lee. In nearly twenty years of research into relationships, however, Lee never found a perfect real-life example of this kind of love. He did find, however, that couples who stay together tend to share the same love style, to fit into the same category. Lee's categories are:

1. *Eros* — love based on physical attractiveness. Quick to ignite, quick to flicker out, and infrequently turns into a lasting relationship.
2. *Ludus* — playful, casual variety of love. Couple engages in gamesmanship and doesn't show high levels of commitment.

3. *Storge* — warmth and affection that slowly and imperceptibly turns into love without fever, tumult, or folly. It emerges from friendship, and is a solid, stable type of love that can withstand crises, but lacks dramatic passion.

4. *Mania* — stormy, topsy-turvy kind of love. Manic lover is driven by powerful urges, particularly the need for attention and affection from the beloved. Manic lover is either climbing a mountain of ecstasy or sliding down a valley of despair.

5. *Pragma* — more level-headed, practical love. Pragmatic lover is searching for the proper mate with a mental checklist of desirable features for the loved one.

6. *Agape* — traditional "Christian" view of love as undemanding, patient, kind, and ever present. More an ideal than a reality.

66. **TRUE**

There are four definite signs of what psychologists call "love readiness":

1. Love is seen as something desirable and rewarding rather than as troublesome or encumbering.

2. There is a longing for inter-personal intimacy and companionship that is not motivated by jealousy for someone else's love relationship or a desire to replace a past love.

3. Sexual frustration.

4. A hopefulness about the possibilities of loving and being loved.

The heart is a brittle thing, and one false vow can break it.

—E. G. Bulwer-Lytton

67. **TRUE**

Such a period of transition is part of the normal cycle of romantic love. The stages in that cycle are:

1. Love readiness
2. Falling in love — ecstasy and euphoria
3. Being in love — optimism, a sense of permanence
4. Love in transition — reality is unmasked by feelings of boredom, impatience, frustration, or hurt. Partners go through a period of testing.
5. Next stage. Either:
   - Mature, long-lasting love; or:
   - Falling out of love

68. **FALSE**

Idealism ultimately destroys relationships, because no human being can possibly live up to another person's expectations of perfection. It's very healthy to counter idealism by taking the time to ponder the following points:

- One of the things I don't enjoy about my lover is . . .
- One of the things that bothers me about my lover is . . .

- One of the things I wish my lover would change is . . .
- One of the things that annoys me about my lover is . . .

69. TRUE

Valentine's Day is a celebration of the emotional side of love. Anyone who doesn't take the opportunity to embrace romance and his/her lover on this wonderful occasion is not a good candidate for the fullest of loving relationships.

70. FALSE

Jealousy can be terribly destructive to a relationship, but so can its absence. Every human being who cares deeply gets jealous at times.

71. FALSE

The word *intimacy* comes from the Latin word *intimus*, which means "innermost, deep." The process of admitting a person into the "deepest" regions of your heart has been called an "approach-avoidance dance." Since we both hunger for and fear intimacy, we come close, back off, then come closer again. The message everyone sends out is "go away a little closer." If you're afraid, you're normal.

Youth's for an hour, beauty's a flower, but love is the jewel that wins the world.

—Moira O'Neill

---

72. TRUE

Lovers should learn from their experiences. If you can't figure out the reasons why previous relationships failed, get some help. Then make sure those reasons won't destroy your present relationship.

Part Three: How Do You Say "I Love You?"

I want not only to be loved, but to be told that I am loved.

—George Eliot

Of all the mistakes made in the billions of relationships between men and women since the dawn of time, number one on the list has to be that oft-repeated assumption, "I don't have to say it. She/he *knows* that I love her/him."

The answer to this so common and so crippling assumption is that what our partners *know* is that love existed when our relationships were born, just as life existed when we were born. But knowing we're alive doesn't mean that every single day we don't crave to reaffirm and savor that life through what we hear and see and taste and smell and feel. Without that sense of wonder, life becomes dull and stale.

Nothing cures like time and love.

—Laura Nyro

Love, too, grows stale, if one or both partners

believes love is something that can be affirmed once, then filed away with other dusty documents like mortgage papers and wills. Like any other living entity, love needs pampering, nurturing, and, especially, sunshine, since in any relationship there will be more than a few days on which rain falls. The sunshine comes not from knowing — but being retold — that we are loved.

Love is the poetry of the senses.

—Honoré de Balzac

Saying "I love you," however, means a lot more than just saying "I love you." High up on the list of mistakes that poison relationships is using those three words as the conversational equivalent of "Have a nice day."

Truly expressing your love, on the other hand, requires making use of the five physical senses — for example, hearing a special piece of music, seeing and smelling a single rose left on a dresser, a taste of caviar and champagne on a special occasion, a touch that says "I'm here and I care" — and that all-important "sixth sense," the anticipation of what your lover most wants and needs at any given time. As Balzac commented, the true poets of love are those to whom words are just one of many tools.

Following, in the third part of the *LQ* quiz, you'll get a chance to find out how much you know about expressing love. The quiz questions and answers should give you a lot of ideas for additional ways in which you can tell your mate how much you care for him or her. As you read, use the blank pages in the back of this book to jot down those ideas.

QUIZ QUESTIONS

T F 73. The best way to express your love on Valentine's Day is by giving a bouquet of red roses.

T F 74. Recording your emotions in a diary can be threatening to your lover.

T F 75. One of the best ways to say "I love you" is to give your mate a photograph of yourself, or even a snapshot of the two of you together.

T F 76. When shopping for your lover, remember the famous quote from the French writer DeColy: "Little gifts maintain friendship; great gifts maintain love."

Of all the music that reaches farthest into heaven, it is the beating of a loving heart.

—Henry Ward Beecher

T F 77. The sum total of "I love you" is not only what you say and do today, but also what you promise for the future.

T F 78. One of the best lover's gifts is something shaped like a heart.

T F 79. The best expressions of love are always those that are completely spontaneous.

T F 80. The best way to discover your lover's idea of a perfect romantic evening or gift is to ask.

T F 81. One of the best ways to say "I love you" is occasionally to treat your lover like a child.

T F 82. Perfume is one of the most overused, boring gifts.

T F 83. When planning time together, always respect your mate's social preferences, whether it be for large crowded parties or quiet dinners for two.

T F 84. One way to express your love is occasionally to take the blame for something that was really your partner's fault.

T F 85. Doing the laundry can be as romantic a gift as a candlelight dinner for two.

One word frees us of all the weight and pain of life. That word is love.

—Sophocles

T F 86. The sexiest gift of clothing is an expensive, revealing nightgown.

T F 87. One sure way to spoil love is to intrude on your partner's fantasies.

T F 88. If you're looking for a different way to say "I love you," try finding a means to express your feelings in every color of the rainbow.

T F 89. Excessive sentimentality can smother even the best relationships.

T F 90. A taste of danger can add zest to a relationship, such as a fast drive on a moonlit night, a raft trip down swirling rapids, or nightcap in a bar in a seedy part of town.

T F 91. Money spent on luxuries such as a limousine rental on your anniversary is better spent on more practical presents.

T F 92. The most romantic men and women are those who use the night for many purposes other than making love.

T F 93. Plan every vacation as if it were a honeymoon.

T F 94. The three phrases that are vital to a loving relationship are "I want you," "I need you," and "I miss you."

T F 95. The rarest and most treasured gift one lover can give another is a lifetime of patience.

T F 96. A measure of love is how much free time you and your partner spend together.

T F 97. The most romantic of gifts are those
           designed to touch the heart.

T F 98. Love letters are old-fashioned.

T F 99. Shouldering major responsibilities by
           yourself is a good way to show your
           affection for your life partner.

T F 100. Your love will be richer if you pack up
           the television set for good.

QUIZ ANSWERS

73. FALSE

There's nothing wrong with sending red roses — a
traditional symbol of love — except that so many people repeat the symbol occasion after occasion, year after
year, until it becomes a meaningless gesture.

Flowers are one of the great love gifts, but they mean
so much more when their full language is exploited.
According to Claire Powell, author of *The Meaning
of Flowers*, the special message of some blossoms are:

Red chrysanthemum	"I love you."
Variegated tulip	"You have beautiful eyes."
Jonquil	"I want a return of affection."
Small daisy	"I love you, too."
Pansy; purple violet	"You occupy my thoughts."
Peach blossom	"I am your captive."
Yellow iris	Passion

White chrysanthemum	Truth
Honeysuckle	Domestic happiness
Red and white roses	Unity

74. FALSE

One of the best ways to show your love is to open yourself completely to your lover. One fine technique is to record your thoughts and feelings daily in a diary — then let your lover read the diary once a month.

75. TRUE

True lovers hold the image of their partner not only in their hearts, but on their desks and bureaus and walls and in their wallets. That's why in love, a picture is worth ten times a thousand words. Those of you who tend to shy away from the camera out of modesty should remember that your refusal to have your picture taken may be interpreted as a statement that "I'm not worthy of your love."

And in the end the love you take, is
equal to the love you make.

—Paul McCartney

---

76. FALSE

The jewelry industry loves this DeColy quote, which has no doubt bankrupted many lovers who have accepted it as true. But sociologists who have explored the dynamics of long-lasting relationships recommend the exact opposite of the Frenchman's advice.

You'll understand why if you think about maintaining love like you think about maintaining a garden. A little attention almost daily keeps the garden vibrant and growing. On the other hand, if you wait until you have the time for a massive cleanup, you'll often find the garden choked, even destroyed, by weeds.

While few lovers would turn down dramatic gifts worth thousands, tens of millions of the richest loves on earth prosper without them. Little gifts chosen with care and presented unexpectedly are the very best of lovers' investments.

77. FALSE

The sum of your love is what you do, not what you promise. While planning for the future is an exciting part of love, excessive promises can only lead to disappointment. If you do talk about the future, make sure you set a realistic goal toward which you and your partner have done some serious planning.

78. TRUE

Good advice for lovers is, when expressing precious sentiments with precious metals, stay close to the heart shape. The most romantic best seller at Tiffany's is the Elsa Peretti "floating heart" necklace.

79. FALSE

You should understand the difference between being spontaneously expressive — being free to hug, kiss, touch, or even let off steam when you need to — and trying to live a totally spontaneous life. The truth is, for most romantic occasions, planning ahead increases the chances things will work out the way you want. Lovers have to be practical as well as romantic. After all, nothing will destroy an evening more quickly than being turned away from a restaurant or hotel because you don't have reservations.

Love: a transitory derangement of all the five senses. The chemistry of attraction.

—Oliver Herbert

---

80. **TRUE**

One of the assumptions most damaging to a relationship is that lovers ought just to "know" exactly what gifts would please their partners the most. You can banish that nonsense by filling in a *Romantic Wish List* that looks something like the following:

- My favorite flowers are

  _____
  _____
  _____

- My favorite colors are

  _____
  _____
  _____

- My favorite scents are

  _____
  _____
  _____

- My idea of romantic restaurants is

    _____
    _____
    _____

- I've always wanted to take a vacation in

    _____
    _____
    _____

- My clothes sizes are

    _____
    _____
    _____

- My idea of a romantic weekend would be

    _____
    _____
    _____

- If you were cooking me a romantic dinner at home, I'd like to have

    _____
    _____
    _____

81. TRUE

Almost all of us have unfulfilled wishes and fantasies left over from our childhood, and nothing would thrill us more than finally having some of these wishes and fantasies come true. As a lover, you should get to know and learn to pamper the child in your partner. Some of the most cherished of romantic gifts include a special doll or a special baseball card desired from youth. Some of the most romantic of moments can come from taking your lover to a place he/she always wanted to go — the Baseball Hall of Fame, Disney World, the ballet.

The sweetest joy, the wildest woe is love.

—P. J. Bailey

---

82. FALSE

The best lovers never neglect the sense of smell. But gifts of fragrance don't have to be limited to expensive perfumes and colognes. Your lover may treasure sachets, potpourris, bouquets of herbs, or single flowers. A scented note is a traditional way to transmit your affection. Bottles or dispensers of perfume or cologne also make terrific lovers' gifts.

83. FALSE

For those truly special occasions — your anniversary and your lover's birthday — you should play it safe and respect your partner's social preferences. But loving also means helping your partner expand his/her social horizons and experiences. A change of pace such as a surprise party or a detour on the way to a big party to a quiet dinner for two can be one of the most appreciated gifts ever received.

84. TRUE

We all know that as responsible adults, we should always take responsibility for our actions — especially our mistakes. Emotionally, though, we can't help fervently desiring to be "let off the hook" every once in a while. Lovers know that, and they express their love by taking turns "shouldering the blame" on those occasions when their partners have just had too much.

It is with true love as it is with ghosts; everyone talks of it, but few have seen it.

—François, duc de la Rochefoucauld

---

85. TRUE

There is nothing more delicious at times than discovering we don't have to do something we dislike or even dread. Realizing that, you should have a written list of the tasks that your lover finds burdensome. Some of them, such as doing the laundry or washing the floors or other household tasks, can be taken on from time to time by yourself. And while you can't relieve all the discomfort of other tasks, such as a visit to the dentist, you can make the experience less unpleasant. Have a bouquet of flowers waiting for your lover at the dentist's office, or pick him/her up afterward for a much-needed glass of champagne and a hug.

86. FALSE

The sexiest gift of clothing is whatever you and your lover find sexy, whether it be a nightgown or a T-shirt or an evening gown or a bathing suit. The most important thing to remember in giving clothing, however, is to show your lover you respect him/her enough to buy the right size and the right style.

87. FALSE

Sharing love means sharing fantasies from time to time. You'll give your lover experiences that will remain vivid for a lifetime if you take the time to remember the fantasies you've heard him/her recite while you're snuggling in bed or walking hand in hand in the woods. For a special occasion, you can go as far as humanly practical to make one of those special fantasies come true. The key here is listening and remembering — you might even want to write them down and put them away in a special "love file" for future reference.

88. TRUE

Most men and far too many women forget that the best way to add color to a relationship is through a gift of something colorful. If you want to accent a relationship, find something to accent your lover's wardrobe or living space. Something colorful can be: a pin or belt or scarf for a favorite dress; a new tie or cuff links or handkerchief for a shirt or suit; a silk flower arrangement for the bathroom; a piece of stained glass to hang in a sun-drenched window; a paperweight for a desk; a vase for a nightstand; a framed photograph of a vivid sunset for the wall.

89. FALSE

Fear of sentimentality is the meanest fear of all. The very foundation of a relationship is built on shared experiences, and no references to those experiences, no matter how sentimental, are unappreciated.

Love between man and woman is really just a kind of breathing.

—D. H. Lawrence

90. FALSE

Mature people express love by showing caution about the person with whom they're in love. Sharing experiences that have an element of risk, such as rock climbing or white-water rafting, is fine if both partners enjoy those experiences equally. But exposing an inexperienced or unwilling lover to any kind of danger — including the danger of sexually transmitted diseases — is the very antithesis of love.

91. FALSE

For those very special nights, penny-wise is pound foolish. If you're going to celebrate, do it right, and that includes a limousine. A Gallup Poll revealed that nearly eight out of ten Americans named a ride in a chauffeured limousine as part of their ideal "romantic evening." That should be good enough for you.

92. TRUE

Which of us wouldn't treasure a lover asking, "May I have ten minutes of your life to watch the sun go down?" Very few. For, while the day belongs to the hectic world of business and family, the night belongs to lovers. The moon nourishes love the way the sun nutures growing things.

Take advantage of the night for romantic adventures — star-gazing walks on the beach, hugging by a campfire, leisurely drives in the moonlight. Every hour spent together at night is another door opened in your lover's heart.

93. **TRUE**

That's a great idea, you say, but it won't work if we have to take the kids along.

Well, you're wrong. What about a bottle of champagne sent up to your room after the kids go to bed, or hiring a babysitter through the hotel so you can have a candlelight dinner in a restaurant overlooking the beach? Vacations are for you, too, and there's always time for the romantic creativity that marked your honeymoon.

Love's tongue is in the eyes.

—Phineas Fletcher

---

94. **FALSE**

Expressing needs and wants is only part — the smaller part — of a relationship. The really important "glue" that holds lovers together are the three phrases, "I'm sorry," "I'm wrong," and "Please forgive me." Each of those phrases, at the appropriate time, is worth a hundred "I love you's."

95. **TRUE**

Woody Allen once remarked, "Showing up is 80% of

life." Nothing could be truer for a long-lasting relationship. The very best lovers are those who show self-control, who wait willingly, who persevere through hard times and unpleasantness, who are fair and forgiving. In other words, the rarest of all finds in a life partner is a person who will give you the ultimate lover's gift — time to work out any problems and right any wrongs.

96. FALSE

Sometimes lovers can suffer more from too much togetherness than from lack of time together. One way to say "I love you" is to give your partner some time alone — perhaps an afternoon to lie in a hammock on the lawn and doze, perhaps a weekend to spend on a hobby, perhaps even a week at a health spa or resort. While lovers may dread separation, they're never afraid of it.

97. FALSE

Sometimes the most romantic of gifts are for your lover's body. You can never go wrong showing by means of a gift that you care for your partner's physical well-being. Great gifts are memberships in a health or sports club, full-day "treatments" at a beauty salon, a series of pre-paid massages, a trip to a special hair stylist, or any other pampering of your lover's body.

Love is never lost. If not reciprocated it will flow back and soften and purify the heart.

—Washington Irving

---

98. **FALSE**

Love letters may be less common in this day and age, but they're not less appreciated. Even if you're the type who hates putting pen to paper, overcome your reluctance in the name of love. No matter how brief the prose or how clumsy the poem, you'll find your missive tucked away in your lover's drawer decades in the future. Absolutely nobody dislikes getting messages of love.

99. **FALSE**

Taking over a minor task your lover finds unpleasant is a great gift. Sharing responsibility for major decisions and problems — meeting bills, buying a house, deciding on a career change, planning for a child — is very important to establishing and maintaining intimacy.

100. **FALSE**

The most romantic of all new high-tech gadgets is the video cassette recorder. Pay a visit to your local video store and stock up on romantic movies for a weekend — old Fred Astaire-Ginger Rogers films, musicals like *My Fair Lady*, great romances like *Gone with the Wind*. Romantic love doesn't fare well in most modern TV series, but the magic of movies on video can whisk you and your love away to the most romantic places on earth for just a few dollars.

What is love without passion? A garden without flowers, a hat without feathers, tobogganing without snow.

—Jennie Jerome Churchill

Part Four: How Much Do You Know About Making Love Last?

A successful marriage isn't a gift, it's an achievement.

—Ann Landers

Few people wouldn't agree that a successful marriage is the supreme happiness life has to offer. So it's very strange that the average American spends more time learning to drive before getting a driver's license than he/she does learning about love before getting a marriage license. And while none of us is foolish enough to believe we can achieve success in our chosen profession without years of hard work and study, most of us expect that success in marriage will automatically drop in our laps.

The result is millions of couples experiencing unhappiness, heartbreak, anger, then divorce. Yet it isn't love that fails — it's people who fail. While no one has ever developed a foolproof, ironclad formula that guarantees a happy marriage for a lifetime, your chances for a successful relationship are much greater if you take the time to study how relationships work, what they mean, and what you can do to enhance or destroy them. Sustaining a long-lasting marriage is an art, and there are techniques that can make you more proficient at that art, just as there are techniques that can make you a better artist or pianist.

We have been poisoned by fairy tales.

—Anaïs Nin

"And they lived happily ever after" is one of the most tragic sentences in literature. It is tragic because it tells a falsehood about life and has led countless generations of people to expect something from human existence which is not possible on this fragile, failing, imperfect earth.

—Joshua Liebman

No matter how practical we are in other areas of life, we've all been bewitched by those fantasies of perfect love we read and watch and hear. We want to believe that falling in love solves all of our problems for evermore and plunges us into a state of eternal happiness. When our real love doesn't match the fantasy, our reaction ranges from disappointment to guilt to outright anger. Then, lacking any real training in organized ways to understand and evaluate our relationship, we resort to improvised trial-and-error solutions that often make things worse.

We pardon to the extent that we love.

—François, duc de la Rochefoucauld

The key to making love last requires banishing the fairy tales of love from our minds, just as we shed our belief in dragons and monsters as we grew up. Then we have to devote the same kind of intelligence and energy to studying about relationships that we devote to our professions or our schooling.

The following questions will help you evaluate how much you know about the dynamics of making love last. And the answers contain facts and techniques that are worthy of lots of study in the months and years to come.

QUIZ QUESTIONS

T F 101. Boredom is the enemy of love.

T F 102. Over the years, long-lasting relation-ships become less stormy and more serene.

T F 103. What your lover thinks of you is critical to what you think of yourself.

T F 104. After a few years of marriage, you should know everything about your partner.

Love is the gentle smile upon the lips of beauty.

—Khalil Gibran

T F 105. People who love each other are affec-tionate in public.

T F 106. The couples who communicate best are those whose communication is the most spontaneous.

T F 107. Doing what's good for you is doing what's good for your relationship.

T F 108. Once a year, you should sit down and formally evaluate your marriage.

T F 109. If your partner acts like a child, you should treat him/her as a child.

T F 110. Marriage partners should understand the difference between mothering and nurturing.

T F 111. Fundamental differences between the sexes mean that a man and a woman can never communicate perfectly.

T F 112. Sacrifice is essential to a long-term relationship.

T F 113. The way to avoid long-term problems in a marriage is to focus your energy on every incident when it occurs.

T F 114. Smart lovers know when to humor or placate their partners.

T F 115. It's possible to have two winners in an argument.

T F 116. A person is headed for emotional trou-

ble when he/she believes that ending a
relationship would be very difficult.

T F 117. In a truly intimate relationship,
partners offer what each one wants
without being asked.

T F 118. Don't be afraid to write a letter to your
lover if you have trouble talking face to
face.

In love there are two things; bodies and words.

—Joyce Carol Oates

T F 119. Aggressiveness on the part of one lover
is a barrier to intimacy.

T F 120. Lovers should put off pursuing individual interests if they're working hard on
improving their communication.

T F 121. The most effective communicator is an
effective listener.

T F 122. When your lover rejects one of your sexual preferences, he/she is really reject-
ing you.

T F 123. Couples should plan for regular "meetings" to discuss problems and goals.

T F 124. Both partners of a marriage feel more

secure when they periodically repeat their formal promise to love forever.

T F 125. One way to find out if your marriage is in trouble is to tune in on what others are saying about your partner.

T F 126. Bringing up the past in arguments helps get rid of built-up tensions in a marriage.

T F 127. Your relationship can be helped by studying couples who are successful at sustaining love.

T F 128. Full self-disclosure is critical to developing an honest, intimate relationship.

T F 129. The pursuit of a career always hurts a relationship.

T F 130. Marriages in which one partner cannot cope with anger are doomed to fail.

QUIZ ANSWERS

101. TRUE

Relationships are sustained by a sense of challenge and adventure. That doesn't mean, of course, that every day can and should be different from the one before — we all have to go to work, raise children, run a household. Rather, we should all try to maintain an adventurous attitude. One way to do that is to try to make just one ordinary moment each day a little extraordinary — flowers delivered unexpectedly, a love note tucked in a shirt pocket, an unplanned intimate lunch in the middle of a hectic day.

True love is the ripe fruit of a lifetime.

—Alphonse de Lamartine

---

102. **FALSE**

All relationships are cyclical from beginning to end. Anne Morrow Lindbergh commented:

> When you love someone you do not love them all the time, in exactly the same way, from moment to moment. It is an impossibility. It is even a lie to pretend to. And yet this is what most of us demand. We have so little faith in the ebb and flow of life, of love, of relationships.

Lovers have to understand that a sudden unforeseen diminishment of desire doesn't necessarily mean rejection or the end of the relationship. Instead, we should wait patiently for the inevitable rhythms of life to restore our lover to us.

103. **FALSE**

The exact opposite is true. The key to a successful marriage isn't finding the right person — it's *being* the right person. Our ideas about ourselves are contagious — when we are feeling good about ourselves and feel irresistible, we somehow manage to convince our partners to feel good about us and to consider us irresistible, too.

104. **FALSE**

There's never any end to the need for openness and understanding in a marriage. No matter how many years we are with someone, we still find ourselves curious. One technique recommended by marriage counselors is to take a moment every day to form one question to ask your lover. Asking a question every day means real communication and sharing never end.

105. **TRUE**

Couples should make a deal — never, never be embarrassed about showing affection in public. Inevitably, one partner is more shy about touching or kissing in public than the other. But over the years, that resistance is worn down, and both partners bask in the glow of admiration others show for their obvious love.

Love is the irresistible desire to be irresistibly desired.

—Robert Frost

---

106. **FALSE**

Communication, verbal and nonverbal, is a skill that must be constantly practiced. The best communicators prepare before discussing an important or sensitive issue in the relationship. Practicing in front of a mirror sharpens nonverbal communication. Talking into a tape recorder allows you to see how the content and tone of your argument sounds from the "other side."

107. **TRUE**

Romance is good for us, and romantics are good to themselves. This doesn't mean selfishness. Rather, lovers should look after themselves physically and emotionally. Physically, we owe it to our lovers to be responsible about our health, diet, and health habits. Emotionally, we must realize that no other person can gratify all our needs and desires — we have to do it ourselves.

108. **TRUE**

Honest evaluations are important in sustaining and improving relationships. Following is one marital self-evaluation quiz adapted from *Time for a Better Marriage*, part of a kit for professional counselors designed by the American Guidance Service.

On a scale of 1 to 5, rate the degree to which you agree with the following statements; 1 means you don't agree at all, 5 means you agree completely:

1. I understand my goals and my partner's goals.
2. I give my partner a great deal of encouragement.
3. I listen to my partner.
4. I can see the positive potential in most life situations.
5. Communication with my partner is open and honest.
6. I am responsible for my own positive self-esteem.

7. I plan and communicate my intentions openly.
8. I am aware of my own beliefs and behavior patterns.
9. I resolve conflict with my partner.
10. I spend enough quality time with my partner.
11. We share home responsibility in a fair manner.
12. We have fun in many different ways.

Scoring:

52-65	Your marriage is mostly positive and satisfying.
44-51	Acceptable score.
28-43	Your marriage needs improvement.
13-27	Both partners are discouraged. You need professional help.

109. **FALSE**

In a marriage, each partner should have the freedom occasionally to pour out raw feelings like a child. While you should listen sympathetically, hard feelings will inevitably result if you react like a parent by lecturing, arguing, or sermonizing.

110. **TRUE**

Nurturing is the mutuality of two people taking turns comforting each other and trying to meet each other's needs. Mothering is one-sided, and can easily result in dependency that eventually turns to resentment.

111. FALSE

Countless marriages have faltered when couples accept old myths summed up in statements such as "That's the way men are" and "That's the way women are." The truth is, what makes a relationship work for both men and women is strikingly similar. Men should realize that everything they want from a woman, a woman wants from them. Women have to be aware that the kind of verbal responsiveness they've received from other women can be available from a man, if they take the time to encourage it.

112. FALSE

Compromise is essential to a long-term relationship. Sacrifice, however, which requires giving up something that is vital to oneself, can lead to damaging dependency.

Two hearts that share one love, one life, will always know true joy.

—Jason Blake

---

113. FALSE

One great secret of successful marriages is to treat all disasters as incidents and none of the incidents as disasters. Lovers should constantly ask themselves, "Is this incident really worth the time for a serious discussion?" In most cases, the answer is no. Real love requires a large measure of mercy. As the Bible says, "Love keeps no record of wrongs."

114. **FALSE**

Your relationship will be much more intimate if you and your partner make a pact never, never to say, "Yes dear." Sustaining love requires paying attention — all the time. It's far better in the long run if you're impolite than to get by by humoring or placating your partner.

115. **TRUE**

The best solution to an argument is for both partners to feel they got "something" out of it. But the most important outcome of an argument is that the issue be quickly and finally resolved. The most damaging disagreements are those that one psychologist calls "round robin rituals," fights over an issue that last months or even years.

116. **FALSE**

Happy couples often attribute the success of their marriage to their shared belief that it is easier to work through problems than to end their relationship. Along with this belief is a shared understanding that disagreements are constructive.

117. **FALSE**

Making the assumption that you always know what your partner wants takes away some of his/her freedom. The motto of a successful marriage should be "Let Freedom Ring." Psychologist Dr. Virginia Satir lists five freedoms that define intimacy:

1. When I can be intimate with you and you with me.
2. When both of us can say what we see and hear instead of what we "should" see and hear.
3. When we can ask for what we want instead of waiting for the other one to ask for it.
4. When we feel what we feel instead of worrying about whether it's the right feeling.
5. When we take steps in our own behalf instead of always trying to keep the status quo.

If love does not know how to give and take without restrictions, it is not love.

—Emma Goldman

---

118. **TRUE**

Writing a letter can be a very effective communication technique. Other keys to good communication include:

- Think through what you want to say and how you'll say it, particularly if it's important or emotionally charged.
- Let your partner know what your priorities are.
- Don't crowd too many requests into one conversation.
- Be concise.
- Don't talk at your parnter. Give him/her time to respond.
- Try not to begin communication by criticizing.

- Ask for feedback to make sure you've been understood.

119. **TRUE**

Other barriers to intimacy include:

- Shyness
- Self-centeredness
- Selfishness
- Lack of empathy
- Conflicting or unrealistic expectations

120. **FALSE**

Pursuing individual interests and maintaining a separate circle of friends are even more important when a couple is working hard on communication. This gives both partners a chance to process the feelings generated in intimate interactions and helps to prevent a psychological overload from too much one-to-one togetherness.

121. **TRUE**

All communication depends on being an effective listener. Some important aspects of the art of listening include:

- Effective listening requires your undivided attention.
- Effective listening is an active rather than passive process.
- Effective listeners are patient.
- Effective listeners avoid putting undue empha-

sis on one word or phrase in a message and wait for the message to be completed before they react.

- Effective listeners don't approach conversations with preconceived notions about what might be said.
- Effective listeners are attuned to their partners even when there's been no request for a discussion.
- Effective listeners understand they don't have to agree in order to listen.

The way to love anything is to realize it might be lost.

—G. K. Chesterton

---

122. **FALSE**

Remembering that sexual preferences have nothing to do with your partner's opinion of you is one key to communicating about sex. Some other important points are:

- Talk with your partner about how and when it would be most comfortable to talk about sex.
- Use books, games, or videotapes to initiate discussions.
- Use "I" language as much as possible when talking about sex, and try to avoid putting blame on your partner for your own patterns of response, or lack thereof.

- Be aware that sexual feelings and preferences change from time to time.
- Don't neglect the nonverbal side of sexual communication.
- Don't expect perfection.

123. **TRUE**

Many couples with successful marriages schedule regular weekly "marriage meetings," for which they prepare an agenda that covers current problems and challenges to the relationship. Some tips about conducting such meetings are:

- Participate as equals.
- Speak honestly and listen empathetically.
- Avoid controversial subjects at first.
- Spend part of the time encouraging each other.
- Don't let meetings become gripe sessions.
- Make decisions jointly.
- Plan an activity for afterward that you both enjoy.

124. **FALSE**

Formal promises of eternal, undying love are part of the "fairy tale" aspect of love that can damage rather than sustain a marriage. Far more valuable is a mutual commitment to concentrate on keeping the marriage alive and healthy. An example of such a pledge is: "We each commit ourselves to working together on the changing process of our present relationship, because our relationship is currently enriching our love and our life and we wish it to grow."

Love sought is good, but given
unsought is better.

—William Shakespeare

125. **FALSE**

One cardinal rule of relationships is: "Always believe
the best about your partner." Participating in gossip,
actively or passively, can erode your confidence in,
and commitment to, your marriage or relationship.

126. **FALSE**

Arguments should always be about the present or the
future, never the past. Dredging up old resentments
and angers can become a habit that destroys any chance
of communicating about the current state of your
marriage.

127. **TRUE**

The key to becoming an expert in any field of human
endeavor involves a great deal of study of those who
are successful in that field. Would-be surgeons watch
skilled surgeons, would-be musicians listen to the fin-
est symphonies, would-be executives pore over case
study after case study in business schools. Yet those
of us who want a long-term relationship seldom think
of taking a look at couples who have succeeded in
staying together in bad times and good. Your study
can even include asking such a couple over for dinner
and drinks — rather than considering your questions

too personal, they're likely to be extremely flattered by your interest.

128. **FALSE**

Honesty is a necessary part of intimacy, but total honesty in the sense of full self-disclosure is not necessarily good for a relationship. The key is understanding the difference between keeping some things private — setting limits on self-disclosure — and outright deceit.

129. **FALSE**

Work and love both require time, but not the same amount of time. No matter how hard a person works, love can still thrive if he/she places great value on sustaining love.

Problems occur when the relationship takes a backseat to a career. One way to prevent that from happening is for a couple to discuss the fact that the world doesn't provide the same kind of acclaim for success in marriage that it does for success in business. An executive who puts together a big deal receives congratulations from colleagues and perhaps a big raise. But no one will give him/her a raise for spending an extra hour a day with his/her kids, or working extra hard on communicating with his/her mate. Married couples have to understand this dichotomy and make sure their values remain consistent within their relationship.

Who are wisest in love, love most, say least.

—Alfred, Lord Tennyson

---

130. **TRUE**

Anger is a valid, if unpleasant, human emotion. A person who is not mature enough to deal with a lover's anger is too immature to sustain a long-term relationship without therapy.

What's Your LQ?

Add up the total number of your correct answers to arrive at at your LOVERS QUOTIENT. If your LQ is:

30-70
You are probably very young or socially inexperienced. You need a great deal more contact with the opposite sex before becoming involved in a long-term relationship.

71-90
Below average. Your relationship or marriage would greatly benefit from serious study of the answers to the quiz questions and the books listed in the Love Bibliography.

91-110
Average. You have experience and some wisdom in love, but you would benefit from more study.

111-120
Above average. You have greatly increased the likelihood of sustaining a long-term relationship.

121-130
You're a genius at love. You would benefit everyone you know by sharing your wisdom and experience.

What the heart has once owned and had, it shall never lose.

—Henry Ward Beecher

Love Bibliography

Blumstein, Philip, Ph.D., and Pepper Schwartz, Ph.D. *American Couples*, William Morrow, 1983.

Branden, Nathaniel, and E. Devers Branden. *The Romantic Love Question & Answer Book*, Bantam, 1983.

Buscaglia, Leo. *Love*, Fawcett, 1978.

———. *Loving Each Other*, Fawcett, 1986.

Fromm, Erich. *The Art of Loving*, Perennial Library, 1974.

May, Rollo. *Love and Will*, W. W. Norton & Co., 1969.

GRIPPING TALES OF

HORROR

THAT SHOULD BE READ WITH *ALL* THE LIGHTS ON . . .

____ **THE HAPPY MAN** — Eric C. Higgs
7701-0422-3/$2.95

____ **THE HIDING PLACE** — J. Robert Janes
7701-0291-3/$3.95

____ **SATAN'S SERVANT** — B. W. Battin
7701-0336-7/$3.95

____ **SLEEP** — Lynn Biederstadt
US/7701-0502-5/$3.50
CDN/7701-0572-6/$4.50

____ **THE WATCHER** — J. Robert Janes
7701-0223-9/$3.95

____ **WIRE-MAN** — Billie Sue Mosiman
7701-0303-0/$3.95

Prices subject to change without notice

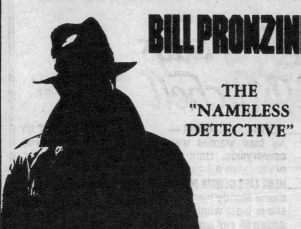

WAYNE D. OVERHOLSER

WESTERNS

___ **BUNCH GRASS** — Chuck Harrigan wanted peace — but he'd have to start a war to get it!
7701-0515-7/$2.95

___ **THE LONG WIND** — Dawson rides off the wind-swept prairie into a fiery war!
7701-0449-5/$2.95

WATCH FOR **GUNPLAY VALLEY**

COMING MARCH '87 FROM

PaperJacks

- -